LE
UPCY
AND LIVE
SUSTAINABLY

The Ultimate Guide to
Upcycling Furniture and
Reducing Waste

By Kirsty Tomlinson

www.upcyclearcade.com 2023

MEET THE MAKER

I'm Kirsty, founder of Upcycle Arcade. An idea, a hobby, and a longstanding desire to create something from nothing became Upcycle Arcade. In other words, I love making things!

I live in a small village in Bucks with my husband and three teenage children. They are used to seeing me in ripped jeans and paint splattered hands.

Some years ago, I wanted some new furniture for our lounge extension, but I wanted 'old new'. I found some lovely pieces which needed an abundance of TLC and my love of being a creative furniture upcycler was born. A little while later, I sold my first upcycled bureau online within 24 hours of posting. I knew then that I was onto something.

I paint furniture every spare minute in my workshop (a converted garage!) I get a sense of achievement with every piece of old unloved furniture that I upcycle so someone will give it a new home and love it again.

I run furniture upcycling workshops for Young Upcyclers age 10-18 and for adults who appreciate a little more detail. These are also available online for both age groups.

Finally, I love writing, be that compliance reports at work or upcycling books at home.

Kirsty Tomlinson

CONTENTS

CHAPTER ONE

Introduction to Upcycling

UPCYCLING IN A NUTSHELL

So, you fancy joining in with the burgeoning boom of furniture upcycling? Great! Upcycling furniture has so many positives:

- Upcycling has a near-neutral carbon footprint. It does not add to the timber shortage, needs very little materials, and requires minimal transportation.

- Old pieces of furniture are often better made than more modern pieces. Dove tail joints are of a better quality than glue and tack. You will find wonderful woods beneath crunchy old varnish, no melamine there.

- Older pieces hold a wealth of history and many stories in their wooden fibers. If only they could talk!

- The 1960s saw a trend of ripping out period pieces, often Victorian artefacts, replacing them with modern alternatives. By upcycling furniture, you'll be preserving a wealth of our heritage rather than resign it to landfill forever.

- You can pick up a wonderful old piece of furniture for very little money. Upcycling is not expensive, it just takes time and a little know-how.

- Once you've mastered some skills and techniques, who knows? This could be the beginning of a pocket money enterprise or a profitable side hustle.

Throughout this book there are pages for you to make your own notes as well as 'to do lists' should you wish. My advice? Jot your own ideas and thoughts all over the book! Do not covet it but use it as a reference and a reminder, including your own experiences and light-bulb moments.

If your book becomes dog-eared, scribbled and paint splattered, then that's a good sign.

By joining the wonderful world of upcycling, you can transform your old and unwanted furniture into something new and beautiful. Upcycling is not only a fun and creative way to express yourself, but also a great way to save money, reduce waste, and protect the environment.

In this book, I will guide you through the process of upcycling your furniture step by step, from choosing the right piece, to preparing it, to applying different techniques and finishes. You will learn how to use paint, apply stencils, choose hardware and more, to create your own unique style. Whether you want to give your furniture a modern makeover, a vintage vibe, or a whimsical touch, you will find plenty of inspiration and tips in this book.

But before we get started, let me tell you why upcycling is so important and beneficial for you and the planet. Upcycling is a form of recycling that involves taking something that is no longer useful or wanted and giving it a new purpose or value. Unlike recycling, which often involves breaking down materials into their raw components and using energy and resources to make new products, upcycling preserves the original form and quality of the materials and adds value to them.

By upcycling your furniture, you are not only saving it from ending up in landfill, but also reducing the demand for new furniture that requires more natural resources, energy, and emissions to produce. You are also saving money by reusing what you already have or buying in old, often cheap pieces instead of buying new items.

And most importantly, you are having fun and expressing your personality through your furniture.

Upcycling is not only good for the environment and your wallet, but also for your health and well-being. Studies have shown that engaging in creative activities can reduce stress, improve mood, boost self-esteem, enhance cognitive function, and promote happiness.

Upcycle Arcade

CHAPTER TWO

Help the Planet

Climate change has been huge news for many years and I am proud to be doing my bit by reducing the amount of good furniture being sent to landfill forever.

Many old pieces have a long history and have often changed hands many times. By upcycling rather than disposing, you are preventing a part of our heritage from disappearing.

New furniture takes a lot of wood (timber) and even if it's been grown sustainably, it still requires a tree to be felled and sawn. Then there's transportation of the wood, often from the other side of the world, to the furniture makers, to the shops, to your home. That's a lot of miles and a HUGE carbon footprint. So why buy new when you can upcycle?

Carbon is one of the most important elements on the planet and if we can create products with more than one life or a continuous cycle of lives, we help extend and ultimately replenish the amount of carbon on our planet. Upcycling is an approach that can help accomplish this.

Plus it is fun!! Humans thrive on creativity. What better outlet to test, develop and use our creativity than re-purposing items that are past their useful life?

"People should always make things whether it's sewing, baking, gardening. Make your own creative environment. It's good for your mental health because you're learning all the time and get a sense of achievement."
Esme Young [Great British Sewing Bee] Simple Things magazine June 2022.

By taking a view that old isn't necessarily rubbish, you really will be making a difference and the planet will be thankful.

CHAPTER THREE

Upcycle? Recycle? What's the Difference?
And does it make a difference?

Upcycling vs Recycling: How to Save the Planet with Creativity

We all know that recycling is good for the environment, but upcycling is better! Upcycling is a form of recycling that involves transforming waste materials into something new and valuable. Unlike recycling, which often breaks down materials into lower-quality products, upcycling preserves or enhances the original quality and functionality of the materials.

Upcycling is not only a creative way to reuse what we already have, but also a powerful way to reduce our environmental impact.

What is the difference between upcycling and recycling?

Recycling is an industrial process that turns used materials into new products. Recycling can be divided into two types: downcycling and upcycling.

Downcycling is the most common type of recycling, which involves breaking down materials into simpler forms and using them to make lower-grade products. For example, paper can be recycled into lower-quality paper, plastic can be recycled into synthetic fibers, and metal can be recycled into alloys. Downcycling reduces the amount of waste that goes to landfills, but it also consumes energy and resources in the process.

Upcycling, on the other hand, is a creative process that transforms waste materials into new products of higher value or quality. Upcycling does not require breaking down or altering the materials, but rather reusing them in their current form or with minimal changes. For example, old clothes can be upcycled into new fashion items, glass bottles can be upcycled into lamps or vases, and wooden pallets can be upcycled into garden furniture or art. Upcycling not only reduces waste, but also adds value and functionality to the materials.

Upcycling vs Recycling: How does upcycling benefit the Planet

Upcycling has many environmental benefits over downcycling.

- Upcycling minimizes the extraction of natural resources. By reusing existing materials, upcycling reduces the need for mining, logging, drilling, and other activities that deplete natural resources and cause environmental damage. For example, upcycling plastic bottles into shoes saves water, oil, and energy that would otherwise be used to make new plastic or shoes.

- Upcycling reduces landfill waste. By giving new life to old or unwanted items, upcycling prevents them from ending up in landfills, where they can take hundreds of years to decompose and release harmful gases and chemicals. For example, upcycling old furniture into new pieces saves space and materials that would otherwise be wasted.

- Upcycling reduces greenhouse gas emissions. By avoiding the use of fossil fuels and electricity that are involved in the production of new materials and products, upcycling reduces the amount of carbon dioxide and other greenhouse gases that contribute to global warming. For example, upcycling old books into notebooks saves paper and ink that would otherwise emit carbon dioxide during their manufacturing.

Upcycling is more than just a hobby; it is a lifestyle choice that reflects your values and beliefs. By choosing to upcycle, you are choosing to respect nature, conserve resources, reduce waste, and create beauty.

Upcycling is not only good for the planet; it is also good for your soul.

Is OLD the new NEW?

Can mis-matched furniture and accessories sit stylishly alongside new?

Style your home with what makes YOU happy

I LOVE new things. Not necessarily in a materialistic fashion, but the gleaming, room transforming change of new. I love new things; things that are new to ME.

A piece of furniture is very often a small permanent fixture; sometimes it has always been there through countless generations. But then suddenly sentimentality looses out to fashion. The age-old loved sideboard is no longer "on point". It remains that loved, cherished piece; often tactile, much knocked and disregarded although still wanted. But it does not fit.

Bureaux (or bureaus...) are my penchant at Upcycle Arcade. I love them. The neatness, the practicality but above all else, the history of their unchanged design for so many years. Desktop computers with separate keyboards struck the death knoll for bureaus but they have seen an enormous revival since working from home became the new norm for many.

Now is not the time for never-ending matching "1980s Laura Ashley chintz". Blending in rather than matching is my preference. An ancient dressing table from a great aunt can be whirled into a splendid statement piece of family history with a lick of paint and imagination. It becomes new...old new. With a story. This dressing table was a wedding present for a young lady waiting for her fiancé to return from the trenches in 1918 and had remained in the same family ever since. New paint, new knobs but the same family heirloom nonetheless.

You CAN keep that heirloom sideboard and still buy a new sofa

The same goes for trinkets and nick-nacks. I have some new ornaments and vases in my home, jostling for prime position alongside my charity finds which I buy because I like, not because they match. I also have some lovely pieces from my Grandparents. They are not worth much, but they are valuable to me. With furniture, someone else's heritage can become yours but in different clothing, setting out on a new journey.

It's not always easy to have the foresight and imagination to see how to redecorate and refurbish your home, room by room, working out what needs to be new and how to embrace your existing old. If you need new walls, woodwork or tiles, you are likely to need a professional

So that old-fashioned family heirloom, that piece which you can't part with but can't bear to look at either, between us we can make it new. After all, old is the new new.

CHAPTER FIVE

Interior Design with Upcycling at its Heart

Scrolling through glossy home magazines can evoke dreams of transforming your own castle into an equally welcoming and alluring showroom. Unfortunately, they frequently feel a little out of reach and altogether unlikely. However, with a dream in your heart and a little imagination in your head, it's amazing what can be achieved with what you already have with occasional help from the flourishing secondhand market.

Let's start with your lounge. There are two things which are not so easy to change without cost and upheaval: the walls and the floor. Walls can be disguised with pictures, and large or hanging plants. The floor can be smartened up with a rug or two – all available on Facebook Marketplace, Gumtree etc. Even the plants!

Almost everything in this picture was not 'new', floor, curtains and sofa being the exception. It was all collected, recycled and revamped and did not cost the earth.

Charity shops, online secondhand sellers, jumble sales, your local recycling center, and [seasons permitting] car boot sales are perfect places to pick up extremely good quality curtains for a song. If they are not to your colour, you can dye them. Bit messy and you must read the instructions, but it works and dye is cheaper than buying new!

Even the cushions have been salvaged from the local recycling centre. Sewing, Needlepoint, Embroidery; these age-old skills taking hours of work, were hidden behind dusty glass or fire screens. With a little imagination these once-loved, long-forgotten pieces are now fit to grace any home of any style and will last for many more years.

See Chapter nine for more ideas on finding a piece of furniture to upcycle.

The same corner but with different upcycled furniture and pre-loved accessories. A little vision and know-how plus a reasonable amount of time set aside, and your home can feel new without the tension and worry of raiding the savings.

New' secondhand settees are always on sale but you will need to factor in transportation plus ensure they are fire retardant. Failing that, a throw (casually draped over, not tucked in with hospital corners) and some cushions really can smarten up your furniture.

A Country Modern look is not all chintzy florals and farmhouse pine shabby chic (I really do not like that phrase). It can be refined yet comfortable, easy to live with. The emphasis is simplicity with natural finishes such as wood, cottons and linens, burnished metals and rustic weaves.

Soften the edges with greenery. Plants freshen the room and the surrounding air. And as I always say, make room for your favourite trinkets, your treasured nik-naks. They will make your showhome your home. Finally, lighting. Ceiling lights are for practical, utility use only as they are, in the main, bright and harsh. Small lamps add a warm glow rather than a stark enlightenment. These can be picked up for a couple of quid secondhand but do ensure the wiring is intact.

Introduce Cottagecore into your bedroom décor. It is the celebration of an idealised rural life.

Cottagecore values traditional and crafting skills with an emphasis on the wholesome purity of the outdoors. It values simplicity and the soft peacefulness of the pastoral life as an escape from the dangers of the modern world. And why wouldn't you want that in your bedroom?!

Your bed and bedding may need to stay put but once again, a throw or a foot-of-the-bed runner will change the look of your bed and with a couple of cushions, who wouldn't want to jump in?

Do you need some storage? Go to the recycling center charity shop and most days there are chests of drawers crying out for an upcycle. Try Facebook Marketplace or the other online shops. You do not need to pay much.

Similar to the country look, think blousy blooms sunny yellows and greens with gingham checks and floral fabrics. Pick up a paintbrush and give your existing furniture a makeover.

This bedroom suite was from Argos - and it looked like it. However, once it had been refinished with a fresh warm grey, it looked anything like flat-pack. Upcycling allows you freedom to push any conservative boundaries you may harbour.

Upcycling doesn't mean painting everything. Clean up and refresh your wooden furniture entirely or part refresh / part paint to make it feel worthy of your room. These are just a few suggestions on how you can give your home a spring makeover whilst being very kind to your pocket and on the planet simultaneously.

Old fashioned dark wood or even newer MDF furniture can be upcycled and looks great once you've injected a little of your personality into it. It looks great AND NEW. New to you.

Upcycling is not just an eco drive, it's a saviour of our heritage albeit with a bit of make-up and a whole lot of bling to boot.

CHAPTER SIX
The Varying Guises of Upcycled Furniture

If you think of upcycled furniture as a colourful slick of paint with some new matching knobs, then you are a missing out on the burgeoning trend which comes with a big sustainability thumbs up.

Bureaus - Take an ancient, old fashioned, beaten up grimy bureau. Chances are it will look downtrodden in most homes. However, once upcycled, it can become a striking statement piece in any colour and any design to settle in any home.

Perhaps that is not to your taste and prefer something a little understated, somber, more unisex and less summery.

Drawers - A chest of drawers can be subdued and gentle or they can be bold and striking. Upcycling is certainly not bland.

Cabinets & Sideboards - What a wealth of choice there is to take a utilitarian practical piece of useful storage furniture into a new stratosphere!

From a classy and subdued sideboard to the hutzpah and decadence of a cocktail cabinet, upcycling gives it all; certainly more than you would find in a furniture retail shop.

Working from Home? It needn't be plain and utility. Opt for Opulence!

before — this is
this is after
Amateur
Professional

It took a lot of time and effort to undo this previously upcycled attempt! But do not let this dissuade you.

If you feel inclined to try your hand at upcycling, do your research such as read this book or enroll in the Upcycle Arcade school of Furniture Upcycling, learn the tricks so you don't go shopping for a tin of solvent based gloopy gloss!

Learn to upcycle furniture in a weekend

Online Furniture Upcycling Course

CHAPTER SEVEN

Is Upcycling for Me?

As previously mentioned, upcycled furniture is on a popularity roll. If you're after an unusual statement piece with added 'wow' worthy of discussion, then upcycled will tick every box. However, a classic and conservative professionally upcycled item can bring understated refined elegance to your home.

Most homes are not graced with bold, colourful artisan pieces of furniture and many homeowners would not want here to be.

Purchasing new furniture can be very costly and quite often the quality does not live up to the price tag. Furthermore, there is a shortage of timber in part due to a boom in housebuilding and a breakdown in the supply chains. A huge benefit of upcycling is the durability and longevity of the furniture unlike much of the new furniture available.

Additionally, with upcycling, you will likely end up with a totally unique piece that you will not find anywhere else. You're probably going to be the only one you know who has one just like it, unique to you and your home.

Upcycling is environmentally friendly. When you upcycle a piece of older furniture, you're not contributing to any environment-harming business practices in the creation of new furniture, its transportation over many miles or adding to the timber shortage. You are also depriving landfill of that old piece of furniture – some 22 million pieces of furniture are thrown away in the UK each year*.

Why not upcycle one of your existing pieces of old furniture to match your own home's aesthetics and décor? Not only is it likely to be cheaper than replacing with a new item, you will be supporting sustainable living with next to no carbon footprint.

Upcycled furniture is not just bold and gold; it is also gentle, plain, conservative, simple, matching and blending.

ESSENTIAL TOOLS

A toolbox is a great and inexpensive gift to receive!

SCREWDRIVERS

A flat (slotted) head has a simple straight flat tip. Get a small and medium size.
A cross head, or Philips, has a cross X tip.

MASKING TAPE

Cheap as chips (£1 for a 5 pack roll) is OK but for furniture painting, you'll want low tack tape to minimise risk of pulling the paint off the furniture. Frogtape Yellow is a favourite but over £5 a roll.

PLIARS

They have flat, typically serrated surfaces, used chiefly for gripping small objects or bending wire: They are also good for gripping stuck bolts holding the drawer knobs in place.

MISCELLANEOUS

A craft knife just £1 from The Works is great if you need a clean edge to your masking take. Often better than scissors. 50cm metal ruler.

CHAPTER NINE

Module 01: Find Your Piece

IF YOU'VE NEVER UPCYCLED OR EVEN PAINTED FURNITURE BEFORE, PICK A PIECE OF FURNITURE YOU ARE PREPARED TO TAKE A CHANCE ON.

IF YOU FOLLOW THE GUIDELINES, AND THINK CAREFULLY ABOUT WHAT YOU'RE HOPING TO ACHIEVE, YOU WILL TRIUMPH.

Find Your Piece of Furniture to Upcycle

One of the most exciting parts of upcycling is finding the perfect piece of furniture to transform. You might already have something at home that you want to give a new look, or you might need to go out and hunt for it. In this chapter, I will share with you some of the best places to find cheap or free furniture that you can upcycle, as well as some tips on how to choose the right piece for your project.

Where to Find Furniture

There are many sources of furniture that you can explore, depending on your budget, preference, and availability.

Recycling centres are places where people can drop off their unwanted items, such as furniture, appliances, electronics, etc., for recycling or disposal. Some recycling centres have a section or a charity shop where they sell some of the items that are still in good condition or have potential for reuse.

I found my pine chest of drawers, which feature throughout this book, for only £5 at my local recycling centre charity shop.

Recycling centres are great places to find furniture that is sturdy, durable, and made of natural materials, such as wood, metal, or glass. You can also find some unique and vintage pieces that have character and charm. However, you might need to visit several recycling centres and check them regularly, as the stock changes frequently and the quality varies. You will also need a vehicle to transport your furniture, as recycling centres do not offer delivery services.

Charity shops sometimes sell furniture, especially larger ones that have more space and resources. Charity shops are another good place to find furniture that is affordable, good quality, and diverse. You can also support a good cause by buying from charity shops, as the money goes to help people in need.

However, like recycling centres, you might need to do some research and visit different shops to find what you are looking for. You will also need to arrange your own transportation or pay a fee for delivery.

Online platforms such as Facebook Marketplace, Gumtree, eBay, Freecycle, etc. are convenient and easy ways to find furniture that is cheap or even free. You can browse through thousands of listings from the comfort of your home and filter them by location, price, condition, style, etc.

You can also communicate with the sellers directly and negotiate the price and delivery options.

However, online platforms also have some drawbacks. You might not be able to see the furniture in person before buying it, so you have to rely on the photos and descriptions provided by the sellers. You might also encounter some scams or dishonest sellers who try to rip you off or sell you faulty or damaged items.

Therefore, you have to be careful and cautious when buying online and always check the reviews and ratings of the sellers before making a purchase.

The most expensive piece of furniture I have bought was for me; a vintage chest of drawers doubling as my bedside table. I had 75cm width to play with and had a clear idea of era and style. After a while of searching, I found the perfect piece on eBay and luckily the local seller was passing my village so dropped it off.

Well, it was the right style, the perfect size but it was thick, really thick, with muck, grease and heaven knows what else. The cleaning, sanding and ultimately covering every once-grubby inch in primer took infinitely longer that the actual upcycling.

Lesson: even the hardiest upcyclers can get duped so keep your wits about you. Happy ending though, I love my drawers!

Garage / yard sales are where people sell their unwanted items from their homes or garages. Garage sales are usually held on weekends or holidays and advertised through signs, flyers, or local online posts. These are fun and social ways to find furniture that is cheap and varied. You can also haggle with the sellers and get some bargains.

However, garage sales are also unpredictable and inconsistent. You might not know what you will find or if you will find anything at all. You might also have to compete with other buyers who are looking for the same thing as you. You are most likely to need a vehicle to transport your furniture.

How to choose your furniture

Once you have found a source of furniture that suits your needs and preferences, you need to choose the right piece of furniture for your project. Here are some factors that you should consider when choosing furniture:

Size: The size of the furniture should fit your space and purpose. You should measure your space and the furniture before buying it to make sure it will fit where you want it to go. You should also think about how you will use the furniture and how much storage or surface area you need.

Shape: The shape of the furniture should match your style and vision. You could look for furniture that has a simple and basic shape that you can easily modify or embellish with different techniques and finishes. However, furniture that has many curves, angles, or details might even enhance your creativity. But don't be put off by the challenge!

This rocking chair was indeed a challenge. Mixing the paint to match exactly with the Cornishware pottery was an afternoon of trial and error then ensuring enough was mixed to complete the whole chair.

But most time was spent thinking: working out how to get perfect stripes at the front then 'bending' them over the top and around the curvy back. A challenge, yes. A triumph? I'll let you decide.

Material: The material of the furniture should be suitable for upcycling and durable enough to last. You should look for furniture that is made of natural materials that can be easily painted, sanded, glued, drilled, etc. You should avoid furniture that is made of synthetic materials, such as plastic or laminate, that might be difficult to alter or damage easily although these pieces are still prime for upcycling.

My own small porch was nothing but a dumping ground for my kid's shoes and bags. But I took a basic IKEA faux wood eyesore of a shoe cabinet and gave it the wow factor with avenues of trees and little multi-coloured houses.

It can be seen through the glass door as you come down the stairs and has returned the porch to a functional storage space with a piece of quirky upcycled furniture.

Condition: The condition of the furniture should be good enough to be upcycled and not too damaged or worn out i.e. beyond your woodworking capabilities. You don't want to spend more time and money fixing a piece of furniture than upcycling it.

You should look for furniture that is structurally sound and functional, with no major cracks, splits, or breaks. Do not be put off by furniture that has minor flaws or imperfections, such as scratches, dents, stains, or chips. You can fix or cover these up with your upcycling techniques.

You should avoid furniture that is beyond repair or unsafe to use, such as rotten, warped, or infested with pests as these may be deal-breakers.

By following these guidelines, you should be able to find a piece of furniture that is perfect for your upcycling project.

Upcycling allows you the freedom to push any conservative boundaries you may harbour.

GOAL OF THE DAY:

NOTES

TAKE ACTION

CHAPTER TEN

Module 02: Preparation

FAIL TO PREPARE; PREPARE TO FAIL!

BEFORE YOU CAN START PAINTING AND EMBELISHING YOUR FURNITURE, YOU NEED TO PREPARE IT PROPERLY. PREPARATION IS A CRUCIAL STEP THAT WILL ENSURE THE SUCCESS AND DURABILITY OF YOUR UPCYCLING PROJECT.

IN THIS CHAPTER, I WILL SHOW YOU HOW TO CLEAN, SAND, AND IF NECESSARY, PRIME YOUR FURNITURE, AS WELL AS LET YOU KNOW WHAT TOOLS AND MATERIALS YOU WILL NEED.

Prepare your Furniture for Upcycling

Preparation Keypoints

Cleaning

 Before you do anything else, you need to clean your furniture thoroughly. Cleaning your furniture will remove any dirt, dust, grease that might prevent the paint from adhering well. It will also reveal any flaws or damages that you might need to fix or cover up later.

Remove existing wax. If you plan to use any paint brand other than Annie Sloan Chalk Paint™ then you will also need to remove any wax. You can tell if there is wax on your furniture by gently dragging your fingernail over the surface, and it will collect underneath.

 You can remove this with mineral spirits. Mineral spirits are like white spirit but kinder to the planet and your hands with less fumes and unwanted scent. Wipe over and use either fine grade wire wool or a scouring pad to remove the wax. It is not the best part of upcycling but necessary as your new paint will not adhere correctly to any residual wax and will spoil the entire piece. *Remember this is not necessary if you are using Annie Sloan Chalk Paint™.

To clean your furniture, you will need:

- A bucket of warm water
- A mild detergent, such as washing-up liquid
- A sponge or a cloth
- A soft brush or a toothbrush
- A towel or a rag

✅ Wash down the entire surface of your furniture. Use the brush or toothbrush to scrub any hard-to-reach areas or stubborn stains.

✅ Remove any hardware, such as knobs, handles, hinges, etc., from your furniture. If using Annie Sloan Chalk Paint™ then you may choose to keep the doors attached and paint them in situ, hinges and all.

✅ You can either keep your knobs and handles for later or replace them with new ones. If you plan to keep them, remember where you stored them. I've lost many a hinge due to putting everything in a 'safe place'.

Repeat until you are satisfied your piece is clean.

✅ Air dry your furniture or use a towel or rag. Make sure there is no moisture left on your furniture.

✅ De-greasing your furniture is easy using either a sugar soap solution (very cheap at hardware or DIY stores) or TSP Alternative from Fusion Mineral Paint. Again, if you are using Annie Sloan paint, this step is a nice-to-have rather than a must-do.

✅ Inspect your furniture for any flaws or damages, such as cracks, splits, chips, dents, scratches, etc. You will need to fix them, see later.

Sanding your furniture

If you are using Annie Sloan Chalk Paint™ you do not need to do any more preparation as it has excellent bonding properties. However:

- You must remove any flaky bits of old paint or varnish by gentle sanding.
- If your piece of furniture has a high sheen or slippy laminate finish such as an IKEA piece, a gentle 'scuff sand' will remove the shine and give the paint something to adhere to, a key. (Just enough to <u>rough up</u> the surface rather than <u>remove</u> the surface).

If you are using other types of furniture paint such as acrylic or eggshell, you will need to do a little more sanding to smooth out any rough or uneven areas and create a very slightly rough surface that will help the paint stick better.

To sand your furniture, you will need:

- A sandpaper or a sanding block with a fine grit, 180 or 240 is enough.
- A dust mask
- A vacuum cleaner or a brush

Use the sandpaper or sanding block to lightly sand the entire surface of your furniture. Follow the direction of the wood grain and apply even pressure. Do not sand too hard or too long, as you might damage the wood or remove too much material. For laminate, a gentle swirling sanding action will adequately remove the top sheen and dull the surface a little.

Use the vacuum cleaner or brush to remove any dust from your furniture. If you are using acrylic or eggshell paint, wipe off any remaining dust from your furniture using mineral spirits otherwise a very slightly dampened cloth will do.

Check your furniture for any spots that you might have missed or that need more sanding. Repeat steps 2 and 3 until you are satisfied with the result.

Priming your Furniture

Not all furniture requires a coat of primer. Many furniture paints have built in primer and topcoat. However, very old, dark furniture or even bare pine can show brown smears through your paint. These are called tannins and are like oils within the wood. Some old furniture can release tannins when water-based paint and wax is applied.

Pine is also rich in tannins plus the dark knots in the wood can sometimes show through pale paint.

To minimise the tannins bleeding through, try not to remove too much the old covering of the furniture. If it's been previously varnished there's little prep necessary as the old varnish will keep the tannins locked in. Scuff-sanding high shine will not break the seal; just go careful not to get too sand-happy.

A primer/cover stain can remedy bleed-through but it's annoying if you have already painted your piece and the tannins put in an appearance. You'll have to sand it smooth, prime well then start again.

There are plenty of good water-based primers such as Zinseer Bullseye (bit pricey). However, sometimes an oil-based primer is necessary and Zinseer BIN shelac primer really does cover all. But DO NOT use your expensive brushes as you will have to throw them away once you use BIN (their cleaner is not tough enough for fine furniture painting).

Do not fight the tannins; manage them.

To recap, priming your furniture will seal the wood and create a smooth and uniform base for the paint. It will also prevent any stains or knots from bleeding through the paint and improve the coverage and durability of the paint.

If you decide that you do not need to prime your furniture, skip the rest of this section.

To prime your furniture, you will need:
- A primer that is suitable for your type of paint and wood
- A paintbrush or a roller
- A paint tray or a container – if you line with aluminium foil, you can re-use the paint tray multiple times.

☑ Cover your work area with a protective cloth to protect it from spills and drips. I use old duvets and sheets as newspaper will stick to wet paint.

☑ Stir the primer well before using it. Do not shake as that will introduce bubbles which will make your furniture, well, … bubbly!

☑ Pour some primer into the paint tray or container, dip the paintbrush or roller into the primer and wipe off any excess, do not overload with primer otherwise you risk having drips or build up along the angles and sides of your furniture.

☑ Apply a thin and even coat of primer over the entire surface of your furniture. Use long and smooth strokes and avoid overlapping or leaving gaps.

☑ Let the primer dry completely according to the instructions on the label.

☑ Check your furniture for any spots that need more primer or that have drips or runs – these will need to be sanded out.

☑ Apply a second coat of primer if needed.

☑ If you are using smooth paint such as eggshell or mineral, sand in between coats with a very high grit such as 400.

Masking Off your Furniture

The next step is to mask off the areas you don't want to paint with low-tack masking tape. This will help you create a neat and professional finish and avoid getting paint on the parts that should remain unpainted.

You should mask off the following areas:

☑
- The inside of the drawers: You don't need to paint the inside of the drawers unless you want to or have to.
- The edges of the drawers: You should paint a small strip of paint along the edges of the drawers that are visible when they are closed. This will prevent any gaps or wood showing through. However, you should not apply too much paint on these areas, as it might make the drawers stick or difficult to open and close.

To mask off these areas, use a pair of scissors to cut pieces of masking tape and stick them along the edges. Make sure they are reasonably straight and smooth out any wrinkles or bubbles. Press firmly – this may seem an obvious step but of you don't smooth the masking tape down, you risk bleed through from the paint.

You have now prepared your furniture for upcycling, a blank canvas for your creativity to shine.

PREPARATION CHECKLIST

Your finished piece of furniture is only as good as the prep you do before you get the paints out. It's mucky and dull but absolutely essential.

Have permission to paint your piece of furniture!

Protect your workplace with old (the older the better) sheets. Protect yourself with old clothes. Paint will probably stain.

Fix it! Ensure any loose or wobbly bits are secured and left to dry.

Clean it! Warm soapy water, inside, outside, topside and underside. All of it.

Degrease it! If your piece of furniture seems a little greasy and grimy and the soapy water isn't shifting it, use a degreaser such as Sugar Soap to remove the grease. Paint won't stick to grease.

Let it dry.

Sand off flaky old varnish, sand smooth sharp or damaged bits of wood. Sand with the grain meaning follow the lines of wood grain. If you sand across the grain, you will break the fibres. Check earlier for information about sandpaper - you need to read that!

Scuff sand (just a gentle sanding all over with a 180 or 240 grit sandpaper) to remove any high shine otherwise there's no need to sand.

Wipe off all dust with a slightly damp rag.

If not planning to paint, remove hardware, door and drawer knobs, even actual doors and hinges if needs be. Remember to store all bits and pieces safely so you don't lose them.

Mask off any bits not to be painted, to smarten up the insides of the carcass.

Turn your piece upside down so when you start painting, you can reach the bottom of the feet, legs or plinth.

SANDPAPER

The lower the grit, the rougher the sandpaper.

80 GRIT

Very rough, good for removing thick varnish. Will leave the wood rough so go over with 180 grit afterwards.

120 GRIT

Still rough, good for sanding off sharp bits of wood.

180 GRIT

Universal good guy. This is neither too rough nor too fine. Use this to smooth beaten up old furniture feet.

240 GRIT

Perfect for a scuff sand to remove a high gloss finish, giving enough key (grip) for the paint to bond. Rough enough to sand down blobs and build up of paint.

400+ GRIT

A super-fine grit for a super-smooth finish. This is perfect between coats of mineral, eggshell or acrylic paint or topcoat.

GOAL OF THE DAY:

NOTES

TAKE ACTION

CHAPTER TWELVE

Module 03: Hardware

KNOBS, HANDLES, DRAWER PULLS: WHATEVER YOU
CALL THEM, THEY'RE PRACTICAL ADORNMENTS OF
YOUR NEW FURNITURE.

GO BRAVE, GO BLING, GO PRETTY, GO PRACTICAL.
GO LARGE, GO TO TOWN OR STAY SAFE.

ALWAYS YOUR CHOICE.

Choose your hardware

One of the easiest and most effective ways to transform your old furniture into something new and unique is to update the knobs!

Drawer and door hardware are the accessories that add personality, glamour and style to your furniture, and they can make a big difference in the overall look and feel of your upcycled pieces. They can make (or break) the piece with little or no cost.

Knobs, pulls, bars all have the same practical function but how do you choose the right hardware for your furniture?

Knobs or pulls?

Knobs are usually a single piece of hardware, a wooden sphere, a crystal cube, a silver lobster (knobs come in all shapes, sizes and materials). Pulls generally dangle. Many older dressing tables and sideboards have dangly pulls and these can be refinished beautifully to be reattached onto your finished piece costing nothing but time and a little paint or spray.

The furniture designer would have selected the original hardware for a reason. Do not immediately go for the change without considering what you already have. It may just need a refinish.

The pulls on the steampunk drawers and the two pieces on the right, are the originals. One has been painted blue with a touch of antique gold gilding wax and the other two scrubbed and polished with elbow grease and lashings of Brasso.

The pulls on the lower antique drawers are positively ecclesiastical (or even a wheat sheaf?) and deserve to stay put for another 80 years.

The knobs on this dressing table, however, were crying out for a change.

New stone and wood knobs from a small independent trader made this piece extremely pretty and saleable.

Bars or Cups?

Bars are exactly that: two bolts with a long cylindrical rod. Round, square, honeycomb, knurled (great word), bamboo or even peacocks!

Cup handles in brushed nickel or satin brass can shift an antique into modernity but do be careful not to try too hard as it may not quite work, may not fit with the overall style of the piece.

Consider the hardware bolt/screw requirement: a single hole is easier to measure and drill than a two-hole pull or bar.

Mix and match - the grey cabinet drawers on the left have T-bars with a single bolt whilst its cupboard doors have matching two-bolt bars. The centre photo shows satin brass cups on the drawers and neat matching satin brass knobs on the doors.

The photos below showcase upcycling at its best. The bar pulls on the larger art deco drawers are the original 1920s hardware. The smaller gold drawer bars are from Amazon whilst the glorious solid brass peacock handles are new from Reckett and George. In other words old with new, cheaper with indulgent. And they all sit side by side on an opulent office suite of upcycled furniture.

For added information: the large art deco drawers were from 1920s, the desk started life as a dressing table in the 1960s but it had perfect proportions for a narrow office. Finally, the tall boy storage cabinet from Next belonged to a lad who lived down the road. It's amazing what a lick of paint can do - along with courage, imagination and some fancy hardware.

 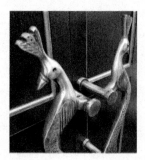 

Heaps of holes

Once you have decided on the furniture hardware, you need to ensure you have holes in the right places and bolts of the correct length to fix the knobs, pulls, handles, bars or cups.

The reason this step is done before you start painting, is so that you can drill new and fill unwanted holes without having to make good your perfect paintwork later on.

If you are replacing like for like insomuch as you do not need to drill or fill, perfect! Easy life just move onto the next chapter.

However, if you plan to change the layout by either changing a knob to a cup or a bar to a pull, then you will need to remove trace of what's already there and drill new holes.

Two-bolt handles come in many 'centre fixing hole' or 'hole centres' with 64mm 76mm and 96mm being the ones I come across most often. Vintage handles follow their own rules it seems so measure carefully the space between the two fixing cavaties.

Measure carefully. Then measure again. If there's a centre hole in a drawer, use that to mark where the two new holes should be. Check the distance from top and bottom is the same for each hole otherwise you will end up with a wonky handle.

Drilling a centre hole is easy as you simply find the centre of the drawer (ruler from corner to opposite corner then mark the middle).

Ensure you want the handles in the middle of the vertical. You may want they sitting a little higher or lower than the centreline. Use your eyes, see how they look. Especially important for cup handles.

Use any wood filler for the unwanted holes. There is no need to fill right the way to the back, just sufficient on the front to give an invisible finish once the dry filler has been sanded back flush.

CHALK PAINT™ FACTSHEET

Versatile, easy to use and fun! Chalk Paint™ is for everyone from casual weekend upcyclers to dedicated furniture restoration artists.

THERE'S NO NEED FOR PRIMING OR SANDING, JUST POP OPEN YOUR TIN, DIP IN YOUR BRUSH AND APPLY THE PAINT TO YOUR FURNITURE.

Chalk Paint™ can be used for a number of different paint effects such as a smooth, modern finish, two colour distress or a textured effect amongst others. Plus Chalk Paint™ adheres to most surfaces, indoors and outdoors, and you rarely need to sand or prime.

Tips and Tricks
- Always stir the paint thoroughly before use as the pigments settle at the bottom.
- On very shiny or glossy surfaces you may want to lightly sand to give a key for the paint to bond with.
- Applying multiple thin coats will also help Chalk Paint™ adhere better.

Waxes and Finishes
- Chalk Paint™ should be sealed with Chalk Paint™ Wax or Chalk Paint Lacquer to protect and finish.
- Always use a lint-free cloth or Chalk Paint™ Wax brush to apply. Work the wax into the Chalk Paint™ (think rubbing in handcream) and wipe away excess before leaving to dry.
- Create a soft sheen finish by leaving for 24 hours and then buff with a very soft cloth.
- Wax will be touch dry within a few hours and cures (hardens) completely in 5-21 days. You can use your furniture straight away but take extra care not to chip or scratch during the curing period.
- Coloured waxes can be used to adjust Chalk Paint™ colours; e.g. dark wax over Emperor's Silk will deepen the red.

GOAL OF THE DAY:

NOTES

TAKE ACTION

CHAPTER FOURTEEN

Module 04: Let's Get Painty!

TAKE THE PLUNGE AND MAKE A SPLASH!

APPLYING THE FIRST COAT OF PAINT HAS TO BE THE BEST PART OF UPCYCLING. YOU CAN SEE YOUR DESIGN BEGIN TO COME ALIVE.

First Coat of Paint

As we have established in earlier chapters, Annie Sloan's Chalk Paint™ is my paint of choice. This step-by-step guide is based on using chalk paint, although the same general 'rules' apply regardless of which paint you choose.

By now you will have prepared your furniture according to your choice of paint and the condition of your piece. You have protected your workspace and have your colour and design decided although you can of course change your mind and simply start again if you're not keen on the results.

Before you start painting, you will need the following materials:
- Chalk paint of your choice. My go-to from day one has been Annie Sloan Chalk Paint™.
- A paintbrush or a roller.
- An old sheet to protect your work area.
- A screwdriver if you plan to remove the drawer knobs or handles.
- Low-tack masking tape to mask off the areas you don't want to paint.
- A supply of cloths to wipe off excess paint or dust. I have cut old sheets and duvet covers into kitchen roll size cloths as an eco and economical alternative to kitchen roll.
- Old clothes!

Paint your furniture with chalk paint

You are now ready for the fun part! You can choose any colour you like, depending on your preference and the style of your furniture. You can also mix different colours together to create custom shades or gradients. Visit Chapter 18 for Inspiration Station if you still need some design ideas.

- If your piece has legs, I recommend you turn your furniture over and paint the legs pointing upwards. This way you can ensure they get an all-over coverage.

- If your piece has drawers, remove them before painting. You have already masked off the side strips to give a neat professional edge.

- Choose between a brush or a roller or a combination of the two (brush for corners, detailed areas, rollers for large expensive sides or tops of furniture). With chalk paint, I usually use just a brush.

- Stir your paint well before using to as pigments tend to settle at the bottom of the tin and separate from the binders over time. Best not to shake as this introduces bubbles which can made painting a little tedious.

- If you are to use a roller, line a small paint tray or even a dinner plate with aluminum foil and pour in some of the mixed paint.

- Dip your brush into the paint by around a third up the bristles, any more then you will have gathered too much paint and you're likely to have drips and runs galore over your piece. Any less and you won't have sufficient paint to spread and it's likely it will dry too quickly leaving immense brush stroke marks. Carefully wipe off any excess on the edge of the container.

- Load the roller with paint then roll it back and forth on the paint tray to evenly saturate the roller. As with the brush, try not to overload your roller.

- Chalk Paint™ is naturally thick and covers well, so a little goes a long way. But aim for two thinner coats of paint rather than a single coat.

- Paint in all directions; here, there, everywhere and as Annie says, every which way. It is a fast way to paint. Aim for an even thickness but try not to labour over one area for too long as you risk dragging your brush through paint that has already started to dry thus creating very textured drag brush strokes. Not a good look.

- Check your progress by looking at your furniture from different angles. Look for drips, build up along edges or heavy brush marks as you go along. Smooth them out gently with your brush or roller while the paint is still wet. Then one last check to make sure you have covered all the exposed areas.

- Paint the top of your piece last as it is more visible and needs a little more attention.

- Let the first coat of paint dry for at least an hour before applying a second coat. If you are short on time or a little impatient, a hairdryer comes in very handy to speed up the drying process.

- Store your brush in an airtight bag. A freezer ziplock, a Shein clothes bag with masking tape over the air holes, or a bread bag but turned inside out otherwise your brush will end up full of crumbs!

Second Coat of Paint

- Paint coat number one must be dry before you start on coat number two. Failure risks coat number one 'lifting' from the furniture as it hasn't had sufficient time to properly bond.

- Scan your piece for drips and build up along edges and if necessary, gently sand these away.

- Coat two is better if a little thinner than coat one. One way is to finely mist the brush with water before dipping it into the paint. A hairdresser's spray (around £4 on Amazon) is much better than a water spray for plants. This loosens the brush preventing it from getting cloggy and claggy. Do not overload with water as the overall finish will not be right.

- You can also lightly sand between coats if you want a smoother finish although this is not really necessary for chalk paint.

- Once you are happy with the coverage, let the final coat of paint dry completely, using the hairdryer again if you wish to help it along.

GOAL OF THE DAY:

NOTES

TAKE ACTION

CHAPTER FIFTEEN

Module 05: Stencilmania

STENCILS AT THE READY!

FOR HANDPAINTED DESIGNS, YOU DO NOT NEED TO
HAVE AN A-LEVEL IN ART.

Choose your stencil

In this chapter, you will learn how to stencil your furniture with chalk paint.

Stencilling is a technique that allows you to add patterns and designs to your furniture without needing to be an accomplished freehand artist. You can take a single design like a monstera leaf and overlay it with another single design frond. Or perhaps a repeat pattern such a Moroccan tile effect in crisp clean lines or weathered and aged.

Stencils are not expensive and are easy to buy.

Tiled, repeat patterns, flora and fauna, words and adverts, geometric, art deco, fun and young, seasonal, retro and love.

You can apply a single colour, layer different colours to achieve a gradient effect or mask off different areas of the stencil to use multiple colours or shades. By using multiple colours, you can create contrast or harmony in your design.

You can keep it clean, gentle and simple. Or you could ramp it up a little by applying some gilding wax to parts of the stencilled design to create an opulent shadow effect. Once you master the basics, let your imagination run a bit wild and try different finishes with your stencil.

Some upcyclers use a sponge or a roller to apply the paint to the stencil and this is fine. However, I do prefer a dedicated stencil brush. A stencil brush is not a paintbrush. Oh no. It's a tough rather solid stocky brush with a very blunt, flat surface. It needs to be much more robust than a mere paintbrush due to the mechanics of applying the paint to the stencil. See later.

have accrued many stencils in my collection. Some are from Annie Sloan which include Scandinavian tiles, Mexican birds, English meadows, or little houses. Some re for children's furniture such as boats and planes, I have highly stylised letters, French advertising, flora and fauna, Japanese cherry blossom, Chinoiserie birds, art-deco fans, retro circles and hearts. And many more including some of my own design which I have had specially made.

Choose a stencil to suit your furniture both in terms of size and your overall desired design and style, one that fits well on the surface of your furniture and does not leave too much empty space or overlap too much either.

A large single shape/object stencil may not seem suitable for a small bedside table but if you are adventurous with your colours, it might work very well. Here there are two overlapped large stencils which show how seemingly over-sized designs can actually work on small furniture.

Choose a stencil that matches or complements the style and colour of your furniture. For example, if you have a vintage-style piece painted in pale neutrals, you can choose a floral stencil in pastel colours for a romantic look. If you have a modern-style dresser painted in black, you can choose a geometric stencil in bright colours for a contrast look. Let the colours pop!

Think eras: is the piece a bit art deco (or would you want it to be)? Are you after a whimsical cottage effect or a Victorian rose? How about a mid-century retro pow? The furniture doesn't have to have been made in the era you're after so open your creative mind to the possibilities.

A repeat pattern covers a large area well. Be aware of having a teensy stencil right in the middle of a large area as it will look lost and disproportionate to the furniture. If your stencil has words, make sure they fit the space without cutting off the beginning or the end. And be ultra-careful that you stencil words the right way up. I learnt that one from experience rather than brainpower.

This stencil was used on my IKEA shoe tidy seen on page 23

Choose your stencil paint colour/s

For this book and in the online furniture upcycling course, I have used a chinoiserie birds stencil and three colours of chalk paint: olive green for the leaves, pinky purple for the birds, and white for the flowers.

Before you start stencilling, you will need the following materials:
- Chalk paint in the colour or colours of your choice. Once again, I use Annie Sloan Chalk Paint™
- A stencil of a suitable size
- A stencil brush
- Low-tack masking tape to secure the stencil
- A wooden craft stick / tongue depressor / large clean lolly stick is very handy

Secure your stencil

Placement is SO important. For a repeat pattern, it is natural to place the stencil top left then work along, moving the stencil as you go. But doing this risks the pattern not looking symmetrically uniform. You will start with a whole stencil on the left and a partial stencil on the right. Not a good look. Same with top and bottom. Find the middle of the surface and the middle of your stencil and start in the middle, working outwards, left to right, top to bottom.

Consider the direction and orientation of the stencil design. With a word or single picture type of stencil, you can work out your placement as you see fit. Place it down, step backwards, step sidewards, check it 'works'.

Taking time to plan your stencil placement will make a big difference to the overall aesthetics of your piece.

The stencil must be secure so to avoid it shifting mid-paint. Obvious though it sounds, it needs to be said. Very low-tack masking tape is ideal but only use tiny pieces, just enough to stop the stencil from going walkabouts. Do not press too hard with the tape as you risk lifting some of your background colour and it is not that easy to fix; not impossible but you still would be better not having to do it at all.

Some books say to use spray adhesive. Personally, I can't risk some of the glue sticking to the background paint or discolouring it in some way. So I don't risk it. You know where you are with tape. Low-tack remember.

Apply the paint

Before you go straight in with the paint, if you are using separate colours for each part of the stencil, mask off areas in advance. For the chinoiserie birds here in the photos, I masked off areas where the white flowers and the purple bird were to avoid contaminating and mixing the colours.

If you plan to blend colours for a graduated effect, masking off areas is not necessary.

Ready? Let's stencil!

Remember: less is more. For a crisp neat finish, build up the layers. Go over the area a few times rather than one thick application.

The stencilling mantra is *Less is More*. It really is.

Too much paint will inevitably bleed under the stencil giving a blurred lie.

Do not dip your brush directly into the paint as you will pick up too much paint. If you have a wooden stick or even a piece of cardboard, decant some paint onto that and pick up the paint from there instead. Not too much, just enough.

Rule do not 'paint' over the stencil. Stipple, dab, perpendicular at right angles to the surface, again and again. Dab dab dab dab. Don't brush.

Build up the colour slowly and you will achieve those crisp lines you're after. A dedicated stencil brush is built for this, flat surface and robust enough to withstand the heavy repeat jabbing motion. Your arm and wrist will ache! But soldier on you must.

Let it dry a bit. Chalk paint is quick drying plus you are applying very thin coats so it will not take long.

Carefully lift the stencil from your piece. Don't drag or slide as you risk smudging your handiwork.

Gently wipe the front and back of the stencil to remove any lingering wet paint as you do not want this paint to splodge on your furniture. Move the stencil to the next section, carefully matching up the design, lightly secure with the tape (reuse old tape numerous times as it's expensive and you don't need new bits each time).

Repeat until colour number one has been applied across the entire area.

Wash your stencil in warm soapy water and let it dry, bone dry. Water is not good on dry chalk painted surfaces as it will mark it. Wash your stencil brush also in warm soapy water and let it dry completely.

A damp brush will thin the paint making it more likely to bleed under the stencil. Use a hairdryer to really dry the brush ready for the next colour.

Repeat the above until all colours have been applied and your stencil design is finished.

Dry brush, dry stencil.

Water is not good on unfinished chalk paint.

To create a gradient effect, apply the first colour, let it dry without removing the stencil then apply the second (and third) colours, gently dabbing over the edges where two colours meet, building up the coverage, creating a smooth transition from one colour to another.

GOAL OF THE DAY:

NOTES

TAKE ACTION

CHAPTER SIXEEN

Module 06: Wax On Wax Off

WAX LYRICAL ABOUT WAX!

PROTECT YOUR FURNITURE AND GIVE IT A VELVETY
SHEEN WITH FURNITURE WAX.

Why wax and what wax brushes

In this chapter, you will learn how to protect your piece of furniture with specialised furniture wax plus how you can add interest to your piece using dark and white waxes.

We will explore how to seal your furniture with wax to protect and enhance the chalk paint finish. Plus it makes the piece durable and long lasting. Wax is a natural product that absorbs into the chalk paint and creates a soft and velvety finish. You will find yourself stroking your furniture as it's warm and supremely tactile!

Unsealed chalk paint will mark and look grubby very easily.

Clean dry hands or close-fitting latex gloves are in order to ensure your pristine paint job stays that way.

Wax also makes your furniture water-resistant and easy to clean. Wax ensures that your hard work lasts for a long time and that your furniture looks beautiful and polished.

Before you start waxing, you will need the following materials:
- I always use Annie Sloan Furniture Wax. It's clean, scent free (unlike some) and beautiful to use. It is also specially designed to work with chalk paint and create a durable and smooth surface.
- A wax brush preferably or a soft cloth.
- A rag or a kitchen roll to wipe off the excess wax.

Choose your wax brush

Wax brushes are made with hog's hair or a synthetic vegan equivalent. Both are equally good. Wax brushes have thick bristles which are tightly packed into a stocky ferrule (the metal part of the brush) with a chunky handle. Waxing is not a delicate pursuit so robust tools are a must.

You can apply your wax with a soft cloth, but I believe investing in a decent wax brush will pay dividends.

There are many types of wax available in the market, but you must select a wax suitable for protecting chalk paint. Annie Sloan Furniture Wax comes in clear, dark, black and white. There are waxes which are shades of wood such as antique pine, driftwood or dark Jacobean etc. but these are for bare wood, not for over chalk paint. (Briwax is a good example of what not to use although I do love it for finishing bare oak cabinet tops and pine tables).

All chalk painted furniture must first be sealed in clear wax with any other shade being applied on top (see later for wax effects).

Remove any drawers – wax them separately.

Swirl your brush in the pot of wax, pick up quite a lot but don't load your brush with too much wax, as it might cause clumps or streaks.

Apply a thin and even coat of the wax in sweeping swirls, almost pushing the wax into the paint. As said before, the wax is absorbed into the paint rather than sitting on top.

Although I've mentioned before 'no hand cream when painting or waxing' apply the wax as if you are applying hand cream. Massage it in, firmly yet gently. Avoid applying too much pressure or rubbing too hard, as it might damage the chalk paint. The paint is textured so you need to swirl in all directions to ensure every ridge of paint is protected.

Wax a section at a time such as a door, a cabinet side. Take a soft, clean cloth or kitchen roll, then gently smooth away any excess wax.

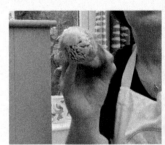

Don't rub or scrub, just hover over the wax and slide from one side to the next. Do not wax half a section then wipe as you may be wiping bare paint, and you are likely to mark it. Wax an entire section at a time before removing the excess wax.

As with the painting, apply the wax on the top of the piece last If you need to wax turned columns, chair spindles or intricate areas, use your fingers to smooth the wax into the paint. It is hand friendly and you can get a lovely coverage this way.

Take care if you have fingernails, I have gouged out many a nick with my nails which then need to be fixed. If you are happy with the finish i.e. with just the clear wax, skip the next step and go to Chapter 16.

Dark waxes add depth, mood, age, contrast and can highlight carvings in your furniture. They come in dark brown and black and can take a flat surface and elevate it to the next level.

But it takes guts and a little confidence to get the most out of using waxes to enhance your piece. Go on, be brave!

Think about what effect you're after. The easiest one to imagine is aging a pale piece of furniture so it stops looking fresh and acquirers some character, some age. You can also increase the depth of really dark paint with black wax. This adds lustre and intensifies the colour.

Before you add any dark wax, make sure you have already applied clear wax. If you add dark wax direct to bare chalk paint, you cannot blend it and you will end up with a horrible dirty smudge. A dollop. Nasty, don't do it. Clear wax first and let it dry a little so it's tacky (don't leave it overnight, but if you do, give your piece a quick slake of clear wax, remove residue and leave until tacky).

Take a fresh clean brush. Another wax brush is good, but I use much cheaper, chiselled 'artist' brushes from DIY shops, solely to apply dark wax and nothing else. Take some dark wax, not too much but be sufficiently generous. And don't be scared! It takes some getting used to, seeing your pristine work covered in thick mud but trust me!

Apply it along the edges or the mouldings which you wish to exaggerate then take your soft, clean cloth and wipe away. If you find you have more dark wax than you can wipe away, apply some clear wax with a cloth or brush which acts as an erasure; then wipe again.

White wax is applied using the same technique, applying layers of wax until the desired finish is achieved. White wax is good for weathering furniture to give a washed-out beach look and works well with pale blues, turquoises and greens.

Stand back frequently to see your piece from different angles and light to ensure your finish is even and consistent. Continue waxing until you are happy with your 'new' furniture.

Clear wax the sides and runners of the drawers to help them glide back and forth.

The wax will be very slightly wet/tacky for a while. Leave it for 24 hours then take a really soft cloth such as a piece of fleece blanket (I have an £2.50 IKEA one which is gradually reducing in size, as I repeatedly cut chunks from it) then buff the wax.

Gently polish the surface – no rubbing or scrubbing – and you will see the surface begin to gleam. This is not a high-gloss finish but a beautiful soft sheen.

GOAL OF THE DAY:

NOTES

TAKE ACTION

CHAPTER SEVENTEEN

Module 07: Finishing Touches

ALL TOGETHER NOW!

Finishing Touches

These last steps are very important. They complete your project and make your 'new' furniture come alive.

So you've cleaned, sanded, prepped, drilled and filled, painted and stencilled, waxed and buffed. Voila! Your furniture is ready for the hardware, new or old, to be attached.

Careful: don't screw your hardware against the paint. In other words, screw the bolt, don't wind the knob. You will gauge out clumps of paint and wax if you do this. Screw on the handle enough to get purchase/hold, push it gently against the surface then with your screwdriver, screw the bolt from the back, effectively pulling in the knob to the piece without it twisting.

Carefully position your furniture - get help if needed. Take care not to lift heavy furniture from just the top as the sheer weight may detach the top from the piece. Support the bottom too. And go easy if you're forced to drag the furniture, small pretty legs may get caught and get wrenched away from the piece. Your floor may get damaged too of course.

Let the wax on the top cure. Wax will fully harden once the moisture content evaporates after around 5-21 days depending on the surrounding atmosphere. Try not to leave waxed furniture too near a heat source or a 365 day super-sunny window. After all, it is wax and extreme heat would soften it a little. Saying that, it has never happened to my furniture but I need to point this out nonetheless.

Dust your furniture with a soft dry cloth but if you need to clean it, use a damp cloth or a very mild soap solution. Do not use any harsh chemicals or abrasive cleaners that might strip off the wax. And don't scrub.

Now you have a wonderful new piece of furniture, painted to your design by your own hand and on a small budget compared to buying new. Plus you have prevented another piece of furniture reaching landfill, another tree from being cut down, another shipment of timber from traversing the planet.

The benefits of upcycling your own furniture are endless. All you need is a little imagination, a spark of inspiration and some paint.

You now have the skills ... so go and Enjoy!

SHOPPING LIST & STOCKISIS

Upcycle Arcade stocks all Annie Sloan Chalk Paint, brushes and accessories*

Annie Sloan Chalk Paint. 120ml £7.95 or 500ml £16.95

Gorilla Glue

Annie Sloan Clear Furniture Wax 120ml £7.45 or 500ml £13.95

Annie Sloan Stencil brushes - £8.95

Chalk Paint brushes - medium £21.95 (available in vegan)

Sugar Soap

Chalk Paint Wax brushes - small £27.95

Masking tape - low tack e.g. yellow Frogtape around £5+ B&Q, Amazon etc

Stencils - Annie Sloan from Upcycle Arcade from £12.95

Sandpaper - Mirka sanding sponges ~£7 pack of 10 from Brewers

Stencils - from Lotties Vintage Home from £8.25

Hobbycraft sticks x50 £1.50

Annie Sloan Paint tin opener £2.95

WHY NOT PURCHASE A PRODUCT BOX FROM UPCYCLE ARCADE? IT INCLUDES PAINTS AND WAX FROM ANNIE SLOAN PLUS ACCESSORIES I.E. EVERYTHING YOU WILL NEED, DELIVERED TO YOUR DOOR. SAVE ON PURCHASING ITEMS FULL PRICE.

VISIT WWW.UPCYCLEARCADE.COM

*prices correct at time of going to print

CHAPTER NINETEEN

Inspiration Station

Are you unsure where to start with designing a new look for your chest of drawers, desk or bedside cabinet?

The Sky is the Limit

Knowing where to look for ideas may just give you enough encouragement to pick up a brush.

You can opt for a windswept beach theme with blues, whites, driftwood; a tropical holiday theme with lush monstera leaves stencilled on a warm sunkissed background; gentle meadow flowers with duck egg blues and sage greens; vibrant boho colour explosion; or art deco decadence with a hint of bling.

Upcycling is an extremely affordable way to get a new look within your home, as striking or a subtle as you choose.

And remember, if you change your mind, you can always get the paint brush back out and start again!

A well-made piece of furniture will look lovely in a single colour be that grey, beige, green, blue, yellow, pink.....

Friends & Family: if you like someone else's decor, think how you can incorporate this into your own home, in your way, with your own furniture and furnishings. A statement chest of drawers designed and painted by your own hand will have other taking ideas from you!

Pinterest: your creativity will be overwhelmed with amazing examples of just how marvelous your piece of furniture can be. There are pins from creators across the globe, each showcasing their talents. You could soon have an arsenal of your own skills. Create a mood board "Upcycled Furniture Ideas". Search tutorials on how to achieve the desired look saved to a new board "Upcycling Furniture Tutorials".

 **Etsy**: furniture painting artisans of all abilities and styles showcase their finished upcycled pieces for sale beautifully.

Search "Upcycled Furniture" for broad results or tailor it to your piece and colour preference "Bedside cabinet painted in duck egg".

Conscious Cubby: like Etsy but solely for UK based upcycled furniture. They promote sustainable living at the heart of their ethos, and this inspired their name.

 **Reclaim & Restore** magazines have the sole intention to motivate you to save waste and to re-use beautifully, the latter publication being dedicated to furniture upcycling.

Colour brochures from paint firms such as Dulux, Valspa (B&Q), Farrow and Ball etc are great, not only for ideas on colours, but they each show rooms with a colour theme and a variety of colour combinations for each.

GOAL OF THE DAY:

NOTES

TAKE ACTION

CHAPTER TWENTY

Shout it from the Rooftops!

Vintage woodgrain oozing rich charm and warmth, soft colours blended like spring clouds or full all-out unabashed opulence. Upcycled furniture has it covered.

Cocktail Parties

A statement piece of bespoke furniture is a focal point for conversation. It's brave, it's different, it's YOURS. Store your spirits and glasses in a kitchen cupboard by all means. But if your collection of gins, rums and vermouths reside in beautifully upcycled history, then you have a piece of wow right there.

Queen of Spades

Drawers and cupboards are nice in creams and greys. They are! But upcycled with gay abandon, they develop their own personality. Add a wild poster with some gold touches, and your brown wooden drawers become an outlet for your inner audacious designer plus are a talking point for visitors.

Welcoming Workspace

Say 'No' to practical utility office furniture and say "Hello Baby" to your very own designer bureau. Faux wood and metal tubes are so corporate. Invest in the cottage industry of upcycled furniture and be delighted and inspired every time you log on. A happy worker is a good worker, is it not?

We wood, would you?

Upcycling isn't all about paint. Bare refinished wood is warm and tactile. Woodgrain is interesting and varied. Take this 100+ year old corner chair, remove years of thick varnish and lo, there's intricate inlay lurking beneath. Coupled with rich vibrant velvet sees old meeting new.

Whether it's a foghorn yelling "look at me" or a coy treasure waiting to be discovered, go bold in a corner of your home, and get the conversation started.

CHAPTER TWENTY-ONE

Cottagecore meets Hipstoric

Over recent years, people have been combining old and new, embracing a more sustainable way of life. Furnishing your home with vintage and inherited pieces alongside modern styles, gives your home a personal, bespoke eclectic interior design.

Hipstoric homes call for vintage décor, and the fusion of modern and antique furniture. Reject the mass-produced and re-imagine vintage and hand-me-down pieces for an individual space. Sustainable living has made the idea of reusing and upcycling even more appealing so take a fresh look at what you already have: will it work with different accessories or perhaps benefit from a more substantial refinish?

Love Pre-Loved

Take a tour of charity shops on the high street, online auctions and freebie sites or perhaps your own loft and you may find treasures that you simply 'like'. A stylish lamp base which when partnered with a new shade, looks wonderfully at home in your home. Does it match? Maybe not. But do you like it, and does it blend with your hipstoric design? Highly likely.

Blend Old with New

Filling a space is one thing but try and make the pieces and decorations complement the space and each other. Even a maximalist approach can benefit from harmony in the design but don't feel obliged to overfill your home as clutter can disarm calm. Just have what you like or need, blending the old with the new!

Refinished, restored or upcycled furniture will effortlessly bring fresh interest to a room without the commitment of a complete overhaul.

"Have nothing in your houses that you do not know to be useful or believe to be beautiful." — William Morris

Cottagecore is the celebration of an idealised rural life. It values traditional and crafting skills with an emphasis on the wholesome purity of the outdoors. It values simplicity and the soft peacefulness of the pastoral life as an escape from the dangers of the modern world.

The Good Life

The ideal became hugely popular on social media during the pandemic. Cottagecore gardening is intended to be environmentally friendly. Think of a garden spilling over with blousy blooms, rambling roses and climbers, native flowers in a mêlée of bee-friendly borders. Patches of pristine lawns turned over to meadow. Attracting pollinators and encouraging biodiversity is the aim of the game.

In Harmony

Lockdown gave many people the chance to appreciate what they have and also to get on board with sustainable living in all or some of its guises. The ideas of Cottagecore and indeed hipstoric design can help to satisfy a desire for "an aspirational form of nostalgia".

The whole ethos of cottagecore and hipstoric design is all a bit idealistic really but it feels nice. It is a welcome comfort to return to when the world is spinning a little too fast as it invariably does sometimes. It helps the busiest of minds quieten down if only for a while.

Harmony and tranquility in spades.

Be a creative entrepreneur

"ENTREPRENEUR: A PERSON WHO SETS UP A BUSINESS TAKING ON FINANCIAL RISKS IN THE HOPE OF PROFIT."

This could be you. You don't have to be an Elon Musk, Bill Gates, a Richard Branson, or a Kylie Jenner to be an entrepreneur. It can be as simple as a desire, a dream; but one you are prepared to act upon.

Where will you be doing your upcycling? Is there somewhere in your home where you can take over for a day or two? Remember to protect all surfaces.

People do buy upcycled furniture. However, many still (erroneously) believe painted furniture should be a bargain because it's second hand. But once upcycled, it's new again. Just a different new.

Upcycling can get mucky

You will need to have the paint, wax (if needed) sandpaper, and paint brush.

If someone sees your upcycled piece of furniture and asks you to upcycle one similar for them, that's a big compliment. But where do you start? Would you do it for free or would you ask to be paid for your creative efforts?

Use the skills you have learnt in this book or on an Upcycle Arcade workshop.

Ask your customer what they would like you to do for them. Plain colours, stencils, gold / silver bling?

Do they have a piece of furniture or an accessory already in mind? If not, you could search for them on Facebook Marketplace, a charity shop, Gumtree, Freecycle or your local recycling center.

Remember it's the little things that can make or break a piece.

Tape off the drawer sides, clean/sand off paint splashes, be neat in your work.

Prepare an estimate of costs for your customer:

o How much the furniture cost you.

o How much did your products such as paint cost? Add it all in, someone had to pay for it at some point so add it in.

o Charge for sundries such as sandpaper, paint brush, paper towels, masking tape.

o How long did it take? Don't guestimate, keep a stopwatch going or download Toggle app.

o What is your hourly rate? For information, the minimum wage for those age 23+ is £10.42 (@ 2023/24).

o Finally, stand back, admire your work and ask yourself one very big question: "Are you giving your customer value for money?" If the answer is yes, then you have your price.

If you are interested in making a few pounds and setting up a business, think about what you want to upcycle whether it's furniture, home accessories (picture frames, vases, boxes), and what your style might be, although this may come over time.

Think about the name of your brand. Take inspiration from this book or from your workshop day, make it memorable. Maybe it tells the potential customer what your business is all about such as Upcycle Arcade (although Apple didn't think like that). Design a logo. Make it yours.

Where to sell is a big consideration. Friends and family are the best place to start. Perhaps Facebook Marketplace, Instagram or even an Etsy shop (free to set up a shop and it costs around 20p to list an item, but they take upwards of 13.5% fees on any sale so build that into your price.)

GOAL OF THE DAY:

NOTES

TAKE ACTION

CHAPTER TWENTY-THREE

Sustainable Living in a Family Home

Energy Efficiency

Reduce energy consumption by making changes to lighting, heating, and window treatments.

Renewable Energy

Explore the use of renewable energy sources like solar panels and wind turbines.

Smart Home Technology

As necessary, incorporate smart home technology to improve energy efficiency and reduce waste.

Reduce and Reuse

Recycling can be a stressful enterprise, so make an effort to minimise waste and conserve resources.

Composting

Start a compost pile or bin to turn organic waste into nutrient-rich soil for your garden.

Semi-Zero Waste Living

A true zero waste lifestyle is unlikely, so do the best that you can to reduce your use of single-use items.

Water Conservation

Implement water-saving measures in your home and reduce water waste.

Grey Water Systems

If you own your home, consider installing a grey water system to reuse water from showers.

Rainwater Harvesting

Collect rainwater to use for watering plants and other non-potable uses.

And upcycle furniture!

CONTACT

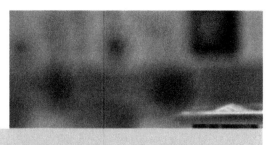

I hope you enjoyed reading this guide to furniture upcycling. Please do let me know how you get on and of course tag Upcycle Arcade in any photos you post out there!

And keep Upcycling!

07546 550087
kirsty@upcyclearcade.com
www.upcyclearcade.com

@UPCYCLE_ARCADE

@UPCYCLEARCADE

@UPCYCLEARCADE

GOAL OF THE DAY:

NOTES

TAKE ACTION

GOAL OF THE DAY:

NOTES

TAKE ACTION

GOAL OF THE DAY:

NOTES

TAKE ACTION

GOAL OF THE DAY:

NOTES

TAKE ACTION

GOAL OF THE DAY:

NOTES

TAKE ACTION

GOAL OF THE DAY:

NOTES

TAKE ACTION

upcycle
arcade

Kirsty Tomlinson

Printed in Great Britain
by Amazon